A Colonial Williamsburg

ACTIVITIES BOOK

Fun Things To Do For Children 4 And Up

By Jean Bethell and Susan Axtell

Illustrations by Alexandra Wallner

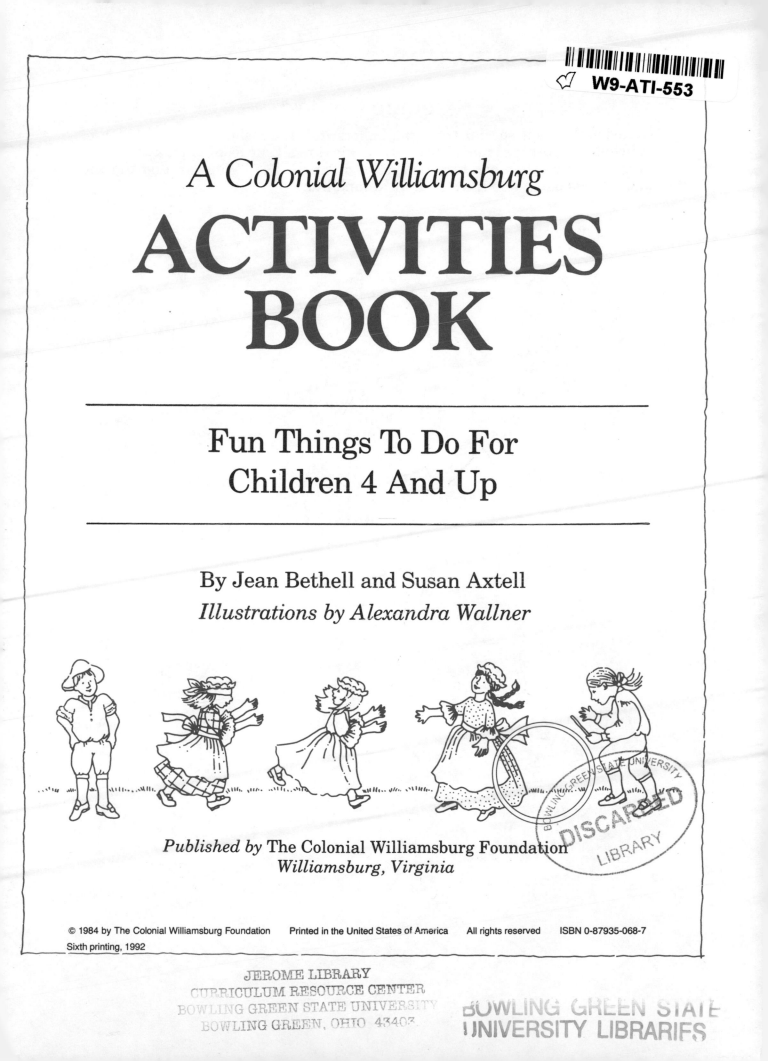

Published by The Colonial Williamsburg Foundation
Williamsburg, Virginia

© 1984 by The Colonial Williamsburg Foundation   Printed in the United States of America   All rights reserved   ISBN 0-87935-068-7

Sixth printing, 1992

Cookie Contest

Occasionally as a special treat the bakers in Williamsburg make a batch of delicious gingerbread men. These big cookies are all supposed to look alike, but every now and then one turns out a bit different. See if you can find the odd man in this batch and draw a circle around him.

Tavern Sign Dot-To-Dot

Here is a favorite tavern sign in Colonial Williamsburg. Follow the dots for the picture.

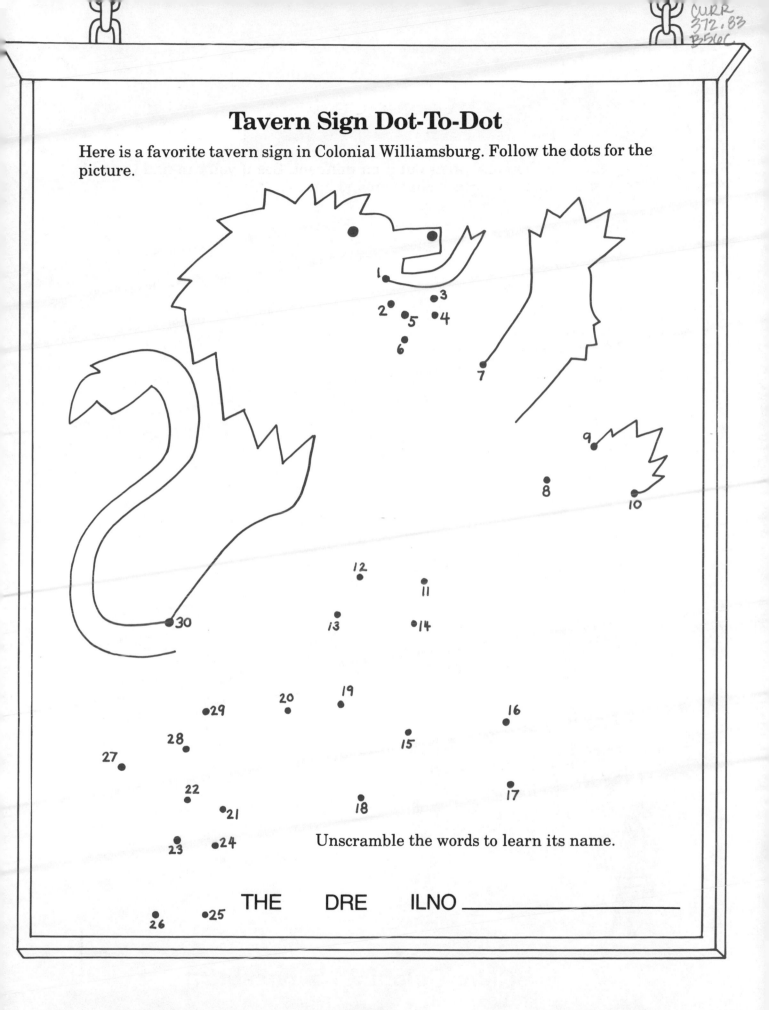

Unscramble the words to learn its name.

THE   DRE   ILNO _____

Color Colonial Williamsburg

This is Duke of Gloucester Street in Colonial Williamsburg. Use crayons or magic markers to color these two pages.

Does this look like a street in your town?

Seek-A-Shape

Have you noticed that many things you see are either round ○ or square □ or shaped like a triangle? △

Take a good look at this picture of soldiers in front of the Powder Magazine in Colonial Williamsburg. There are several circles, squares, and triangles in the picture. See if you can find them. How many are there?

Workaday Williamsburg

Here are some of the people who lived and worked in Williamsburg many years ago. Each one is making something. Draw a line from the person to what he or she is making.

Lock, Stock, and Crossword

In colonial times, people were sometimes punished by being put in the pillory, shown here, or the stocks.

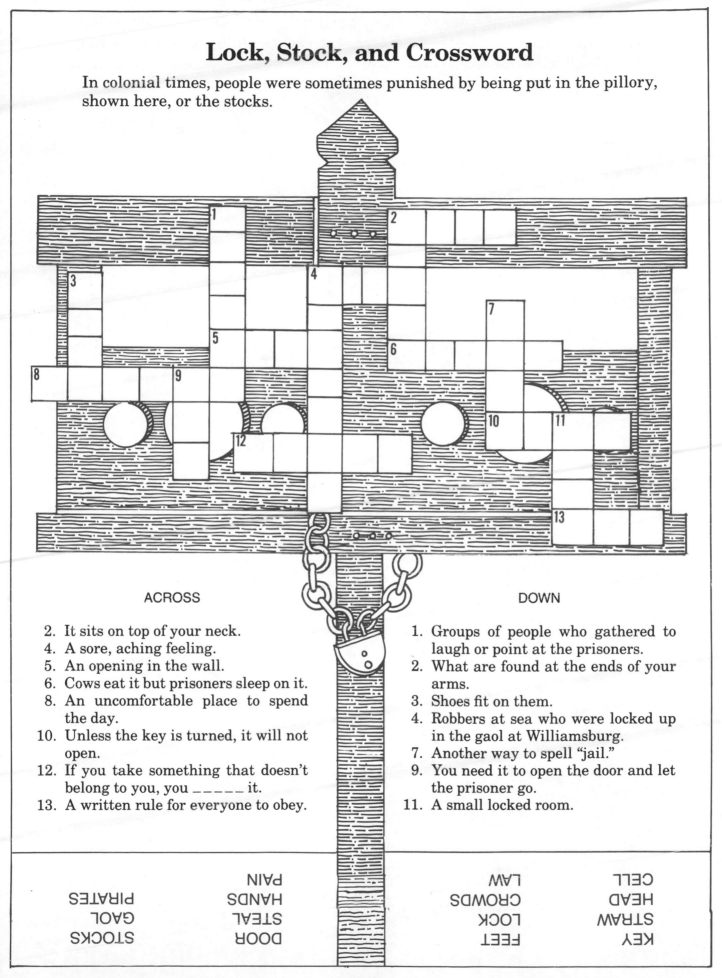

ACROSS

2. It sits on top of your neck.
4. A sore, aching feeling.
5. An opening in the wall.
6. Cows eat it but prisoners sleep on it.
8. An uncomfortable place to spend the day.
10. Unless the key is turned, it will not open.
12. If you take something that doesn't belong to you, you _ _ _ _ _ it.
13. A written rule for everyone to obey.

DOWN

1. Groups of people who gathered to laugh or point at the prisoners.
2. What are found at the ends of your arms.
3. Shoes fit on them.
4. Robbers at sea who were locked up in the gaol at Williamsburg.
7. Another way to spell "jail."
9. You need it to open the door and let the prisoner go.
11. A small locked room.

PAIN
HANDS
STEAL
DOOR

PIRATES
GAOL
STOCKS

LAW
CROWDS
LOCK
FEET

CELL
HEAD
STRAW
KEY

A-Maze-ing Garden

People in colonial Williamsburg loved their gardens. Besides flowers, fruit, vegetables, and trees, some gardens had bushes cut in special shapes that were called topiaries. People also liked mazes.

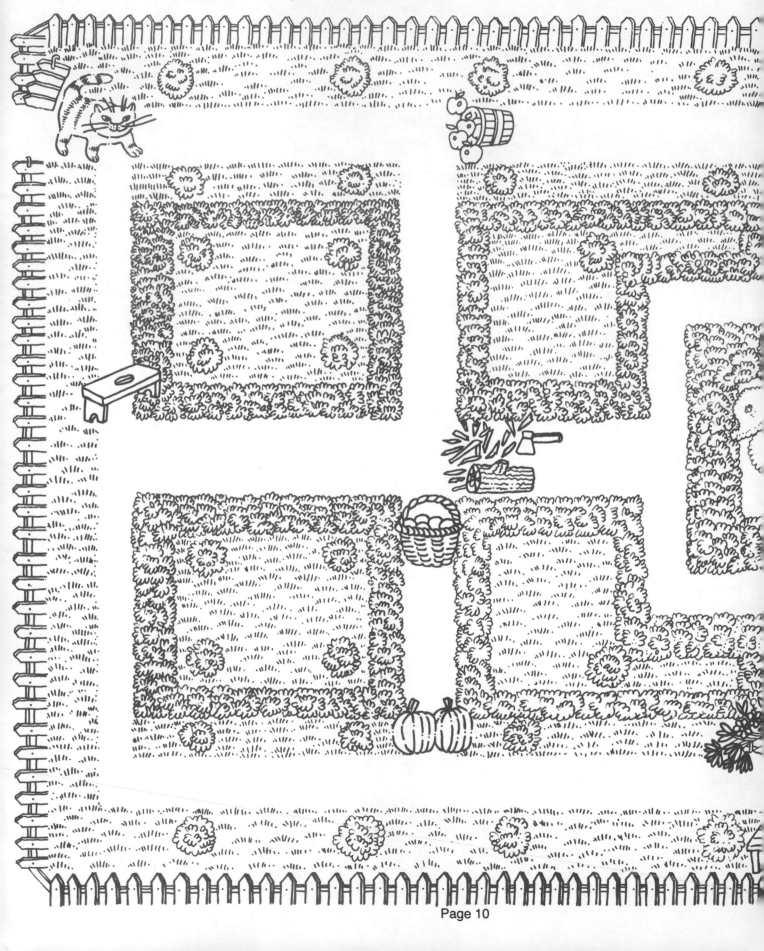

Here in the Bryan House garden, Mrs. Blaikley's cat, Tansy, has come from next door to stalk and catch a robin. But that smart little bird has found a hiding place under a bird-shaped bush! Can you find your way to him before Tansy does?

Alphabetics

Each of the letters of this alphabet is made of something which begins with that letter. All of these things could be found in colonial Williamsburg. Can you guess what they are and color them with magic markers or crayons?

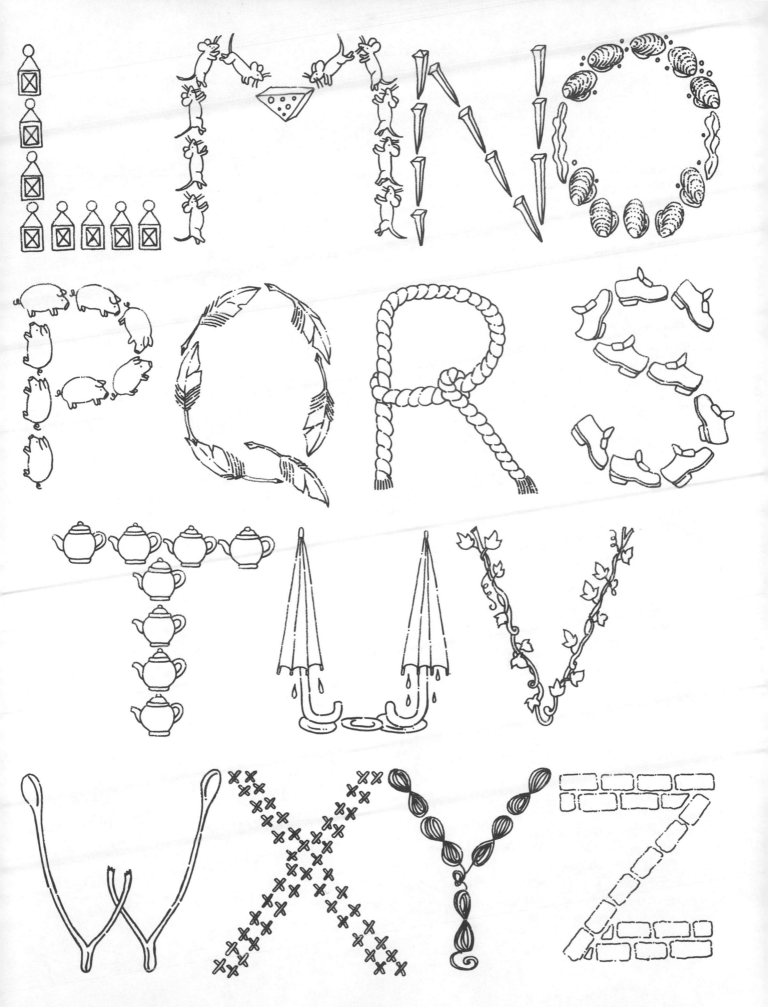

Colonial Cut-Outs

Cut out the fan along the heavy lines. Fold the edge of the paper away from you on the first dotted line (#1). Flip the paper over and fold the second dotted line toward you (#2). Continue flipping and folding (#3 toward you, #4 away from you, etc.) until the fan is finished.

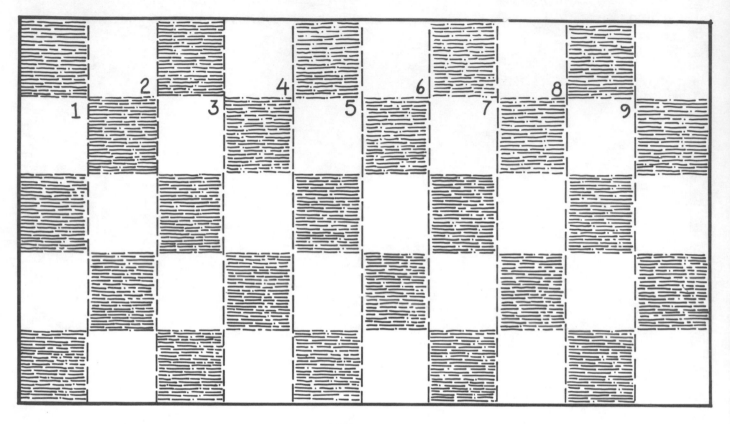

Color and cut out the boy and girl figures. Carefully cut around the leg holes on the dotted lines. Insert your fingers from behind and make the dolls walk or run or dance!

Two By Two

Which two objects make music?
Which two could you use to carry water?
Which two could you ride in?

Which two could you use to cut something?
Which two could you grow in your garden?
Which two could you wear on your head?

Making Things Move

Up and down, round and round, back and forth—all of these Williamsburg people are busy making things move. Put an X beside the ones who are moving things up and down. Put a check by the ones with things that are going round and round. Circle anyone who is making something go back and forth.

A MYSTERY MESSAGE

Here are two shop signs in Colonial Williamsburg that are rebuses, messages written in pictures instead of words.

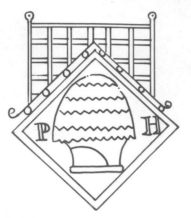

Peter Hay's Shop shows a *hay*stack and his initials.

Hartwell Perry's Ordinary shows a *hart* (another name for a deer), a *well*, and *pear* trees.

If you can read his rebus puzzle, you will have an invitation to join in some special fun.

Shoes That Don't Fit

In colonial times shoes were not made in factories the way they are today. Instead, they were all made by hand by the shoemaker.

You would have found many boots and shoes at the Boot and Shoemaker's Shop on Duke of Gloucester Street in Williamsburg. Here are some kinds of footwear that people might have worn long ago. But 7 don't belong. Can you find them? Draw an X beside each shoe that is out of place.

Mystery Dot-To-Dot

In the field behind the Peyton Randolph House is a building with lots of moving parts. It has "arms" that whirl, a house that can be wheeled around, and stones inside that rub against each other. Connect the dots and see what a wonderful place it is.

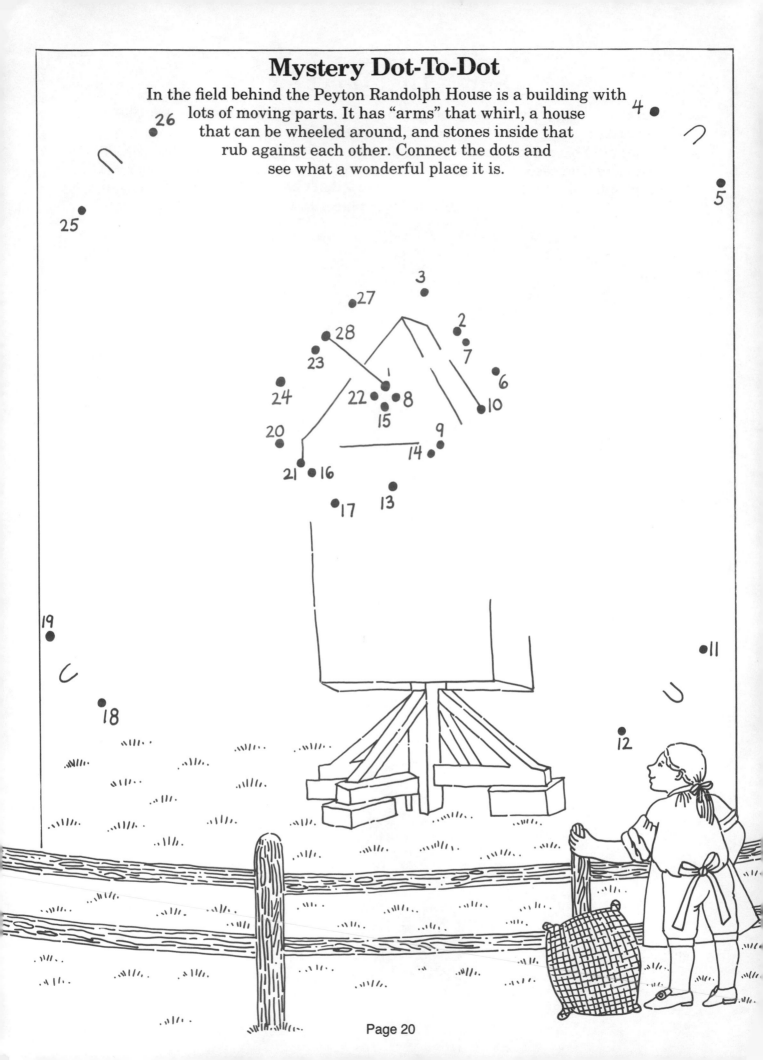

Alphabet Scramble

When you visit the printer's shop on Duke of Gloucester Street, you'll see many trays full of type. The printer will show you how he takes letters from the trays, fastens them together, and rubs ink on them. Then he uses the big printing press to print newspapers and books.

Several letters are missing from this tray of type. Write down the missing letters, then arrange them so they'll spell out the name of the famous Williamsburg building pictured below.

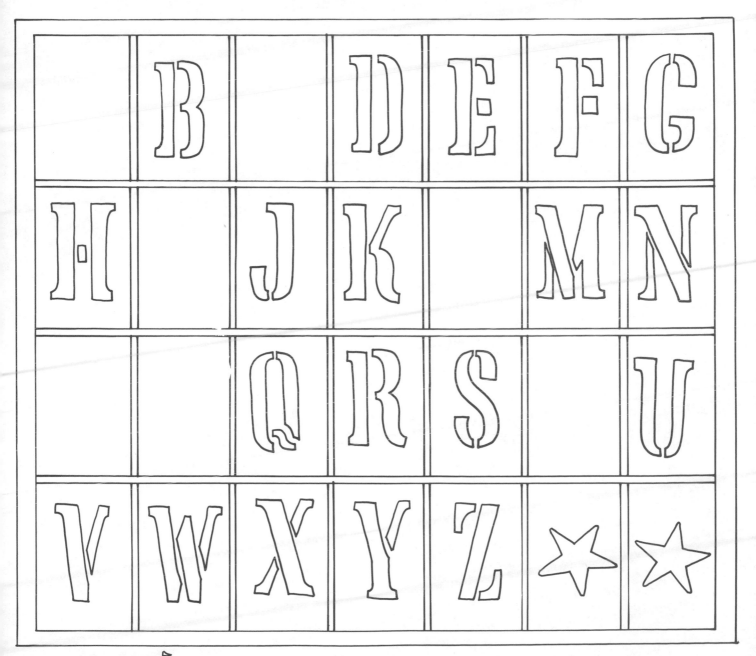

_____

See What You Can "C"

People in colonial Williamsburg worked hard at their crafts and their chores. In the yard of the George Wythe House you can see animals being cared for, household jobs being done, and many useful things being made.

How many things can you find in Mr. Wythe's yard that begin with the letter "C"? Draw a circle around them or point to each.

child	curtains	cock	carrots
chair	checks	cat	cucumbers
crabs	chicken coop	caps	chimney
clothes	churn	candles	cow
clouds	cradle	corn	cart

Fun Search

Here are some things you might do if you were a boy or girl growing up in colonial Williamsburg. See if you can find all of the underlined words in the find-a-word puzzle on this page. Draw a circle around each word.

Would you like to roll a <u>HOOP</u> or <u>RUN</u> a <u>RACE</u> on the Palace Green? You could <u>JUMP</u> over puddles, <u>CLIMB</u> a tree, <u>HOP</u> on one foot or <u>DANCE</u>. You might play <u>TAG</u> or hide-and-<u>SEEK</u> or <u>BALL</u>. Perhaps you'd rather <u>SING</u> or play a <u>DRUM</u>, fly a <u>KITE</u> or spin <u>TOPS</u>. If you were very lucky you might have a special toy to play with—a Noah's <u>ARK</u> or a <u>DOLL</u> made of wood, rags, or cornhusks.

B	P	J	Q	A	W	S	E	E	K	O	B
L	N	U	M	R	U	N	G	H	X	M	Y
R	S	M	U	K	H	I	O	S	I	N	G
T	Q	P	B	A	L	L	P	L	V	J	Z
N	A	I	S	D	A	N	C	E	O	R	P
L	Q	G	N	R	T	B	W	X	E	H	D
G	V	J	A	U	E	R	V	B	H	O	P
D	O	L	L	M	Q	A	M	S	I	O	A
J	U	W	D	K	B	C	K	T	O	P	S
X	H	S	K	I	T	E	M	Q	G	Y	T

Word Harvest

You have probably noticed that there are many gardens in Williamsburg. Since there were no supermarkets two hundred years ago, people had to grow most of their own food.

Here are some of the things they grew in their gardens. Draw a line from each fruit or vegetable to its name. Maybe you'll want to color them too.

PUMPKIN

CHERRY

RADISH

GRAPES

LETTUCE

CORN

APPLE

A Colonial Fair on Market Square

Have you ever been to a fair? Children in colonial Williamsburg looked forward to Fair Days. There were good things to eat, interesting things to buy, and exciting contests, races, and performers to see.

At this busy fair on Market Square can you find the things that rhyme

with FOX   with TAKE
with FAT   with CAN
with BIG   with MUG
with AM

ox, clocks, locks, socks
hat, cat, bat, rat
wig, pig, twig, jig
ham, ram, jam, lamb
cake, rake, snake
man, fan, pan
jug, hug, rug

A Lamb's Tale

Colonial children wore clothes that were made at home. Very few things they wore were bought in a store. What can you tell about the making of their clothes by looking at these pictures?

Who is feeding the lambs?

Who is shepherding the sheep?

Who is clipping the wool?

Who is carding, or combing, the wool?

Who is spinning the yarn?

Who is weaving the cloth?

Who is knitting the socks?

Who is wearing new clothes?

Rhyme Time

Here are some rhymes about people who lived in colonial Williamsburg. Each one of these verses has a blank space at the end. Say the rhyming words and write them in the blank spaces.

Boom, boom—tweet, tweet
Here they come
The boys who play
The fife and _____

These happy people
Danced a jig
But one old fellow
Lost his _____

One boy's skinny,
One boy's fat
But they both wear
A tricorn _____

To write their names
And count to eight
Colonial children
Used a _____

Why is this man
Sad and pale?
The judge has sentenced
Him to _____

Jail   Slate   Hat   Wig   Drum

Page 30

Sign Here!

Many of the shops in Colonial Williamsburg have colorful signs outside to show what is made or sold there. In the eighteenth century, many shops in Williamsburg also had signs.

Here are 7 signs that you might have seen as you walked around town. Match the signs with the things for sale by putting the sign number in the right square. For example, sign No. 1 shows that newspapers and books are for sale inside.

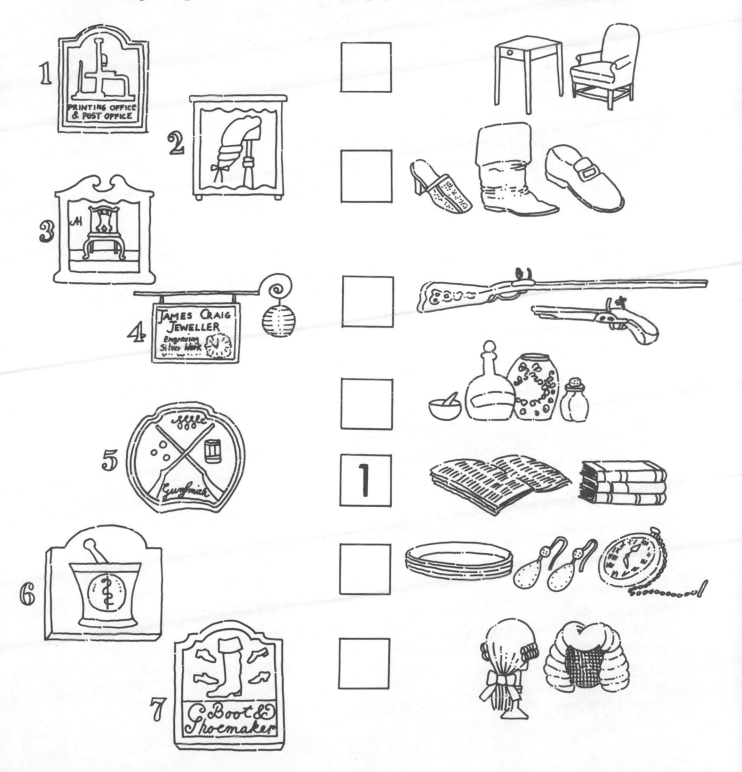

Many toys today are very different from those in Colonial Williamsburg, but some colonial games and playthings are very familiar to us. We can play colonial games using things we have now. Here is how:

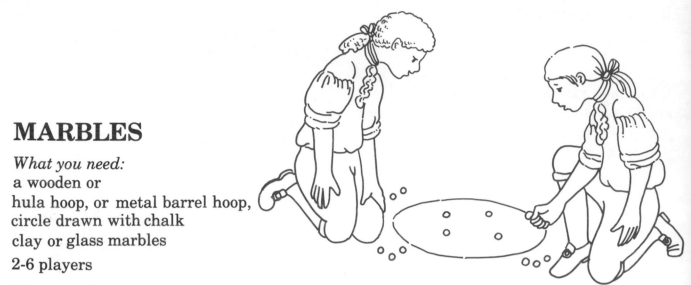

MARBLES

What you need:
a wooden or
hula hoop, or metal barrel hoop,
circle drawn with chalk
clay or glass marbles

2-6 players

What you do:
Place one marble in the center of the circle (hoop). Pile your marbles on the outside of the circle and take turns rolling or shooting. Try to hit the marble in the center. If you miss that marble stays in the circle. Anyone who does hit the center marble wins that marble and any other marbles in the circle. The winner places one marble in the circle and play begins again.

BILBO CATCHER

What you need:
a paper cup
a 12-inch length of string
a button, metal washer, or nut

What you do:
Poke a hole in the center of the bottom of a paper cup. Run the string through the hole and knot it on the inside. A piece of tape over the knot will keep it from pulling through. Tie the metal nut, washer, or button to the other end of the string. Holding the paper cup in one hand, swing the button or nut out away from you and try to catch it in the paper cup. It takes a lot of practice!

BUTTON WHIRLIGIG

What you need:
a medium or large sized two-hole button
a 24-inch length of string

What you do:
From the top side, feed both ends of the string into the button holes and tie the free ends together in a double knot. Center the button along the two string lines. Hold the knotted end in one hand and the U of the string in the other. Holding tightly, twirl the string away from you with both hands (as if you were jumping rope) until the button whirligig is wound up. Pull both ends sharply and watch the button whirl.

TOOTHPICK TOP

What you need:
a round toothpick
a circle of stiff paper or cardboard

What you do:
Trace around a jar top or 50 cent piece to form a circle. Carefully cut it out. Poke a hole in the very middle of the circle and insert the toothpick so that the circle rests half-way down its length. Spin the toothpick between thumb and forefinger and let go. Top spinning takes lots of practice too. Keep trying until the spin lasts.

HOOP ROLLING

What you need:
a wooden or metal barrel hoop, hula hoop, or old wheel or tire
a stick

What you do:
Roll the hoop or wheel away from you, then run to catch up with it and hit it again to keep it moving. See how long you can keep it rolling without stopping. Another way to roll a hoop is to drive it with a stick, hooking the stick inside the hoop, pushing hard to get it going, then running to push it again and again.

Something's Missing!

Here are pictures of some things that are often seen at Colonial Williamsburg. Something has been left out of each one. Be an artist and add the missing parts.

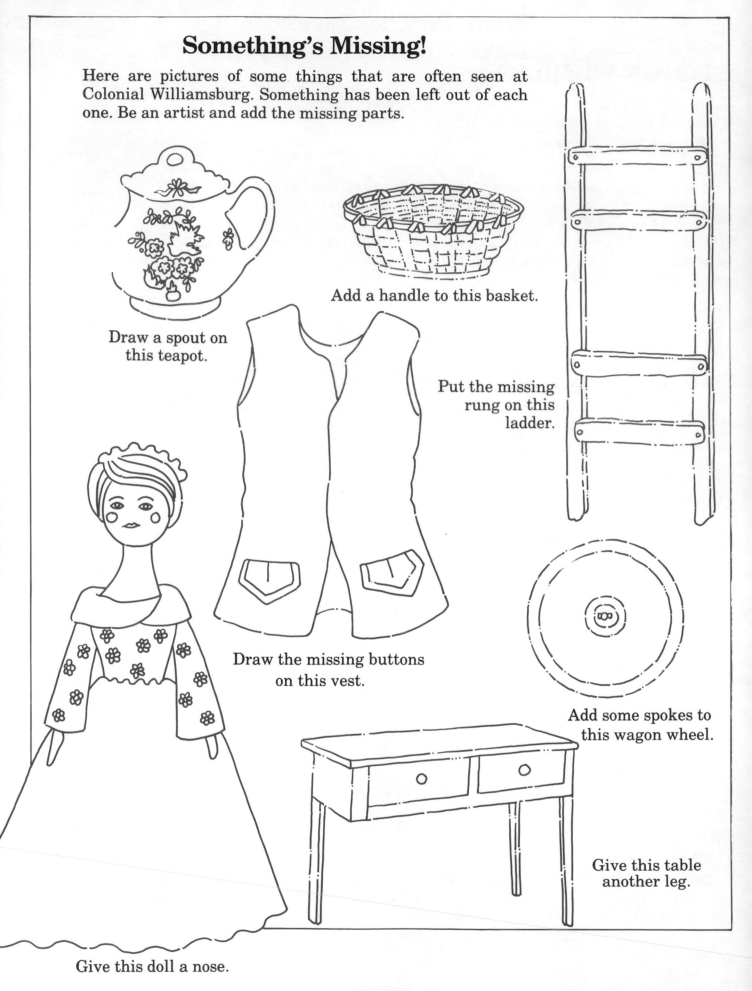

Draw a spout on this teapot.

Add a handle to this basket.

Put the missing rung on this ladder.

Draw the missing buttons on this vest.

Add some spokes to this wagon wheel.

Give this table another leg.

Give this doll a nose.

Where Do They Live?

Can you match the animals you see below to the places where they live? Draw a line to show them the way.

Watch the Birdie!

Birds like to live in big trees like this one. How many birds can you count in the tree? Look carefully. Some are hidden very well!

What Happened?

These pictures tell a story when they are arranged in the right order. What might have happened first? What next? And how did the story end?

Then and Now

Draw a line between what people used in colonial days
and what we might use today.

Then

NOW

Alphabet Dot-To-Dot

Where did people who lived in Williamsburg long ago get water to drink, to cook with, and to wash clothes with? Connect the dots from dot A to dot Z and you'll have a picture that will give you the answer.